Water
Up, Down, and All Around

Written by Natalie M. Rosinsky
Illustrated by Matthew John

Content Advisor: Dr. Raymond M. Hozalski, Assistant Professor of
Environmental Engineering, University of Minnesota, Minneapolis, Minnesota
Reading Advisor: Lauren A. Liang, M.A., Literacy Education, University of Minnesota, Minneapolis, Minnesota

AMAZING SCIENCE
PICTURE WINDOW BOOKS
MINNEAPOLIS, MINNESOTA

Editor: Nadia Higgins
Designer: Melissa Kes
Page production: The Design Lab
The illustrations in this book were prepared digitally.

PICTURE WINDOW BOOKS
1710 Roe Crest Drive
North Mankato, MN 56003
www.capstonepub.com

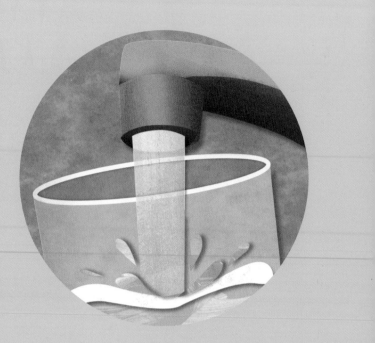

All books published by Picture Window Books
are manufactured with paper containing at least
10 percent post-consumer waste.

Library of Congress Cataloging-in-Publication Data
Rosinsky, Natalie M. (Natalie Myra)
  Water : up, down, and all around / written by Natalie
M. Rosinsky ; illustrated by Matthew John.
    p. cm. — (Amazing science)
Summary: Describes the water cycle and the importance
of water, explaining evaporation and condensation, dew
and frost, and the three states of water.
  ISBN 978-1-4048-0017-5 (hardcover)
  ISBN 978-1-4048-0336-7 (paperback)
  1. Water—Juvenile literature. [1. Water.] I. John,
Matthew, ill. II. Title.
  GB662.3 .R67 2003
  551.48—dc21   2002005734

Printed in the United States of America in North Mankato, Minnesota.
032012   006669R

TABLE OF CONTENTS

Where Do Raindrops Come From?

Plop, plop, splash. Raindrops trickle down your face.

Once these raindrops sailed in a cloud. They roared in a river. They crashed on the seashore.

These raindrops have circled the world.

The Water Cycle

Raindrops are made of water that has been used over and over again since Earth began. They are part of Earth's water cycle.

The water cycle begins as water flows down from mountain lakes. Water also springs up from deep within the earth. From mountains and springs, water runs into rivers and oceans.

Fun fact: Water covers more than 70% of Earth's surface.

Sunlight heats up nature's water until it evaporates. When water evaporates, it rises into the air.

See page 21 for an experiment about evaporation.

Heat turns water into very tiny drops called water vapor. Water vapor is floating in the air all around you, but you can't see it.

Water vapor cools off as it rises in the air. As water vapor cools, the tiny drops get bigger and bigger. The drops can now be seen as a mist or fog.

Watch the clouds sail through the sky.
Clouds are also made of water vapor.

Fun fact: You can see water vapor
indoors, too. Steam is the vapor
that rises when water boils.

When clouds brush against cold air, their tiny drops of water vapor get even bigger. The vapor in the clouds condenses and turns into rain. If it is cold enough, the vapor may turn into snowflakes.

12

Water vapor condenses in other places, too. In early morning, you might see dew glittering on a lawn or field. Water vapor in the warm air has condensed onto the cold grass.

See page 21 for an experiment about dew.

When it is cold outside, frost
sparkles on your window.
Frost is frozen dew.

Where Does Water Go?

Snow melts. Dew drops evaporate into the sky and turn into clouds. Rain flows into streams, rushes into oceans, or sinks silently into the ground. Water gets trapped in mountain ice.

Fun fact: Only 1% of Earth's water is good for drinking. Most water (97%) is salty sea or ocean water. The rest is ice.

How Is Water Used Along the Way?

Deer drink from forest lakes. Fish swim through ocean depths. Corn and wheat grow tall as their roots suck water from the ground.

You need water to live, too. Fill up your glass. Jump in the pool. Rinse your soapy hands.

Fun fact: Earth's water is used over and over again. You might be drinking water that people or animals drank thousands of years ago.

Yuck! Water can become too dirty for drinking or swimming. Unhealthy things can wash into water from factories, farms, lawns, and toilets. That is why cities have places to clean the water people drink.

Not-so-fun fact: Wild animals don't have ways to clean their water.

Round and Round We Go

Plop, plop, splash. Rain dribbles down your boots.

Fun fact: Water dribbles inside you, too.
Your thirsty body is two-thirds water.

The water cycle begins again.

Experiments

Dry Out an Apple Slice: Did you know that apples are made mostly of water? With an adult's help, cut a slice of apple. Let it sit on a plate for several days. Watch what happens to the apple as the water inside it evaporates.

Make Your Own Dew: On a warm day, add lots of ice to a glass of water. Wait several minutes. See how water vapor in the warm air condenses on the outside of the cold glass.

Make Your Own Frost: Fill a plastic bowl with hot water and place it in the freezer. Take a glass or metal plate and put it next to the bowl. Close the freezer door and wait a few hours. What has happened to the plate?

Fast Facts: Liquid, Solid, Gas

Water has three forms. It can be a liquid like the wet water you drink. It can be a solid like hard ice cubes. Or it can be a gas like the hot steam that rises from a cooking pot. Water changes from a liquid to a solid or a gas at different temperatures.

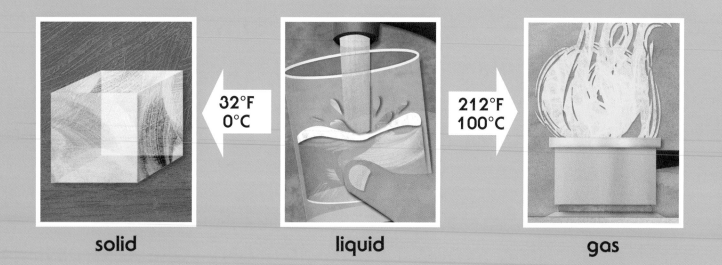

solid   32°F 0°C   liquid   212°F 100°C   gas

Wonderful water is the only thing in the world that can change naturally into a liquid, a solid, or a gas.

Glossary

condense—to change from tiny drops of water in the air to wet water you can see, like raindrops or dew

dew—small drops of water that collect on cool grass and other things, usually outdoors

evaporate—to change from wet water to tiny bits of water that float in the air

frost—a very thin layer of ice

water cycle—how water changes as it travels around the world and moves between the ground and the air

water vapor—tiny drops of water in the air that you can sometimes see

To Learn More

More Books to Read

Fiarotta, Noel, and Phyllis Fiarotta. *Great Experiments with H₂O.* New York: Sterling, 1997.

Flanagan, Alice K. *Water.* Mankato, Minn.: Compass Point Books, 2001.

Hooper, Meredith. *The Drop in My Drink: The Story of Water on Our Planet.* New York: Viking, 1998.

Wick, Walter. *A Drop of Water: A Book of Science and Wonder.* New York: Scholastic, 1997.

On the Web

FactHound offers a safe, fun way to find Web sites related to topics in this book. All of the sites on FactHound have been researched by our staff.

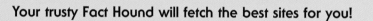

1. Visit *www.facthound.com*
2. Type in this special code: 1404800174
3. Click the FETCH IT button.

Your trusty Fact Hound will fetch the best sites for you!

Index

Amazing Science

Water: Up, Down, and All Around

Steam and frost, raindrops and dew. Vivid illustrations and clear, simple text plunge the reader into Earth's amazing water cycle. Each book includes a glossary, hands-on activities, and fascinating Fun Facts.

Look for the other books in this series:

Dirt: The Scoop on Soil

Light: Shadows, Mirrors, and Rainbows

Magnets: Pulling Together, Pushing Apart

Rocks: Hard, Soft, Smooth, and Rough

Sound: Loud, Soft, High, and Low

CONTAINS AT LEAST 10% POST-CONSUMER WASTE

ISBN 978-1-4048-0336-7

90000

9 781404 803367

PICTURE WINDOW BOOKS
www.picturewindowbooks.com
CAPSTONE PUBLISHERS